FREE VERSE EDITIONS

Edited by Jon Thompson

THE WASH

THE WASH

Kirsti —
thank you
for the bird —

Adam Clay

Parlor Press

West Lafayette, Indiana

www.parlorpress.com

Parlor Press LLC, West Lafayette, Indiana 47906

Printed in the United States of America
S A N: 2 5 4 - 8 8 7 9

Library of Congress Cataloging-in-Publication Data

Clay, Adam, 1978-
  The wash / Adam Clay.
      p. cm. -- (Free verse editions)
  ISBN 1-932559-99-X (pbk. : acid-free paper) -- ISBN 1-932559-
46-9 (adobe ebook)
  I. Title.
  PS3603.L385W37 2006
  811'.6--dc22

                                    2006032305

Printed on acid-free paper.

Cover illustration © 2003 by Kirsti Wakelin

Parlor Press, LLC is an independent publisher of scholarly and
trade titles in print and multimedia formats. This book is available in
print and Adobe eBook formats from Parlor Press on the Internet
at http://www.parlorpress.com. For submission information or to
find out about Parlor Press publications, write to Parlor Press, 816
Robinson St., West Lafayette, Indiana, 47906, or e-mail editor@
parlorpress.com.

for Kimberley

Contents

ACKNOWLEDGMENTS

Grateful acknowledgment is made to the editors of the following magazines where earlier versions of these poems first appeared: *42 Opus; Black Warrior Review; The City Paper; Forklift, Ohio; Free Verse; Good Foot Magazine; Kulture Vulture, The Iowa Review; LIT; The Literary Review; Luna; MiPoesias; The New Orleans Review; Octopus Magazine; Pindeldyboz; StorySouth; Three Candles;* and *Unpleasant Event Schedule.*

I would also like to thank everyone who has helped along the way: Matthew Henriksen, Shannon Jonas, Alex Lemon, Tony Tost, Tara Bray, Brandon Shimoda, Joshua Marie Wilkinson, Amanda Nadelberg, Kate Greenstreet, Geoff Oelsner, Marvyn Petrucci, Davis McCombs, Michael Heffernan, D.C. Berry, Angela Ball, and the late James Whitehead.

Many thanks to Jon Thompson, David Blakesley, Maurice Manning, and Joyelle McSweeney.

Thank you especially to my family.

And to Kimberley, for everything.

The brow of a horse in that moment when
The horse is drinking water so deeply from a trough
It seems to inhale the water, is holy.

—Larry Levis, *"Anastasia & Sandman"*

". . . meditation and water are wedded for ever."

— Herman Melville, *Moby Dick*

THE WASH

SAINTLY

Trusting the rhymes for what they are
The rhymes trust back and break us all

I.

THE MOST CAREFUL MUSIC

[Caught No Fish]

Caught No Fish Last night or night before Last,
Shot an Autumnal Warbler,   —
                 Found its Belly filled with Seeds,
Wrapped them in The Paper in my Sock. The Paper
Has a Line on it, the Length of my Wife's foot
For a New pair of Shoes. The Line leads this Expedition
Home. This Expedition floats Down-river
In Search of a Place to Bed.
                 The Warbler (I was in My Dream)
Gained the Power of Observation, and *If My Eyes*
Did not err, my Own Face as Seen
Through the Bird's was Filled with the Glow
Of A *Church Bell ringing.* Once I Killed a Fish Crow
And hundreds flew to him and appeared as if about to Carry him off.

[OUR HANDS SAILING]

Our Hands sailing all day—the night, a blanket gone black,
The night never known until one is waist-deep in it.

It stains my eyes—the water looks bruised.

Of the faces seen drifting in the wake of our boat,
My Father's stare is the deepest.

This river does strange things to men.

My hands are not my own,
                         The blood runs purple
In my veins—no birds in sight—*the Weather quite rough, all day,*
We have made a bad Landing according to my ideas—

Rocks Inside a Cupped Hand

after Roethke

Pebble or pond in order of importance?
      One holds water,
The other pushes the flow toward a lamb carcass;

                Like wine that hath taken wind
And hollows a hole in the sand,
The pond dries up to a puddle unseen.

The Unknown of the seasons
Remains inside a nest on a curving limb.

              Woods haue their eares,
And fields their eyes; so apt, and able is euery place
To detect close villanie.

Odd and Full of Love

Once along this path it was as if God stirred me
Between the eyes. My head fell from a cloud
To a meadowed land where woodlarks forever search
For twigs too heavy to carry. Upon waking, the stulp
Where I stood was no more. I witnessed beetles moving
Near my face as if for the first time free from the galling glow
Of the sun. Larks reappeared. The song of their hungry young
Sweetened the air. Beetles dropped to their holes,
And I thought of Mary and the many trees
It would take to build a ship to sail to her.
Hourly now a voice asks *Well honest John how fare you now at home,*
And my reply is thrown to the pigs each morn.

WHAT HAPPENED

I caught a bird in this piano. The fearful song,
Flapping wings, strings struck by a feathered body
Rhymed like the curve of a bone bent almost
To break: *Sweet, dead Silencer, most suddenly clear.*

A cracked door let a stream of light in
And the pear I held sucked up the song,
Turned to rot: a small sea, the bursting forth,
The simple commerce of bird and tree.

But the light that showed my face this room
Is a dance no one remembers. If I could touch
That bird right now, if I could eat that pear,
Oceans would be too quiet to remain eternal.

Fetters of ice and blood, I can't sing what I heard:
The history of this room is out of tune.

Whittlesea Mere

The bark men have all gone home. Pails of milk
Wait along the doors to cool in the night,
Reflections of ghosts look up from each one.
Covering cherubim of clouds above,
The boy on the brig has come to the Fens
To find his sister who, he's been told,
Is buried at the feet of a stranger. His mother says
The same words spoken for the named
Were spoken above his twin. The boy kneels and draws
An O on each grave as if to reach through the dirt
And bring her tiny bones up to the light.

Bones and Wandering

The grave of light is now underwater. Scoundrels curve
Around the riverside and laugh so loud it remains night
For three days.

                    This laughter serves to cover up
Their true purpose: searching to remedy the curse
Of their contorted faces.

Even the trees seize up and become savage
In this strange dark. Even the map lies about the valley
Where the river scours.

                    Hands black from all the blood and dirt
This river once washed away. Those gathered here
Wish to drag something, they know not what,
From the rift into which they stare.

ELEGY

I took cold water from the river in my hands, drank,
And looked down to see a rock black with the memory of my face.

REFLECTION ON IDLENESS

A shoal never before seen, the center of the world
    From where everything reaches out.

Mosquitoes blocking out the sky—

River dried up, *fatigued of being* Idle *so powerfull*
Are habits of all kinds that to spend
A Month they would render me sick of Life—

What of idleness? What of the rain which over us does pass?

A week gone by.

A violin and its music do much to guard the mind
Against idleness. Its song can flood the river.

Notes on the Constraints of Architecture

The only thing more frightening than the abyss
Is oblivion's lie,
The thought that the abyss,
That great rent of nothing,
Might not be.

This doesn't bring terror to you in sleep,
But it does remind you to focus

On that which you can see—
That which you know to be real.

One example: The circle of light

Moving down the wall onto the bed

Through the hole in the curtain
Above your part of this large room.

You wake just as the light
Reaches the plate of your face
So that it burns your vision

And all you see is white.

This daily moment is your thorn.

And you have known many thorns.
You have known how thorns

Can expand the limits of one's flesh:
How thorns can resist restraint.

As a child you were unseen on the streets.
You barely saw yourself in a puddle

And an angel watched you from a tree
As you turned away from the distorted image
Of what you thought your face had become
And what the water showed it to be.

This room has no mirrors, only paintings.

The birds in these paintings look back at you
As if they were your reflection
Or you were theirs.

You feel drawn to the paintings
And think of the tree, the woods,
The birds, while touching the frames.

The splinter in your hand has been there for many days.

At night the stillness of frames both comforts and terrifies.

And the mornings, rarely varying,
Are filled with the most careful music of all:
The human voice. No
Piano or cello can remain as heavy as the words
Collecting in the corners of this large room.

They do not go away.

You see things said last month, last year.
They all merge and become an abyss of infinite possibilities.

They make the room so white
That you walk on your shadow.

I know you are not puzzled by light or the lack of light
For the transient are asleep in the past,
Waking in the present, and dying in the future,

So what is it that confounds you?

It is the blur between everything you've written
And everything you've read?

You claim it all as your own and rightly so.
No one here wishes to take that from you.

Instead, the memory of the Giant Forms
Will be on your face each time you wake.

Those in the room will see a vision of what was once there.
In their faces you will see a blurred reflection of your past.

You will continue to forget the velocity of your own songs.

II.

The Tongue of a Bear in Your Pocket

DREAM OF THE PATH
FROM ESSEX

Four days with no birds, empty nests everywhere,
and I expect the void to stretch farther
than sound into the next year. The idea of a bird
will not come near either, but the sky falls nightly
around my voice and this song is mine no more.

WHAT THE BIRD THOUGHT

The line from Heidelberg to Paris did not leave until nearly midnight.
A sparrow flew onto the train as we were finding our seats,
and two of the French rail-staff laughed as though this occurrence
was a sign of our deserved place among the unfurling threads
of eternity. I laughed too, but not to agree with their observation.
My laugh was an apology for the collision of thoughts
inside the bird's mind. The train began to move and the bird flew
down the aisle of the car searching for air on the other side of the window.
A hymn cannot exist in fury or in silence without a god to hear it.

TINY ECLIPSE

Born into a beehive of clarity, bedtime and endtime
are the laugh inside a shotgun barrel,
the space of air between undoing the holy and tucking desire
into itself until it *is not so.*

But it was. And what once was
is. Some still look to the sky for the next curse.

A heron appears to fall.

Slight rip of light, the valley where salt water pools,
the bird in the grass, wings stretched, tiny eclipse
of feathers and bones. Perhaps the curse has taken
on a bird-like form. Grubs dance in the dirt. An empty
birdbath waits in the twig-colored dark.

THE PULL

Hidden in the hedges, the man means no harm.
His terrible eyes do not look through the window
where a child dreams of falling into light
and a fan trembles circles in the thick air.

The smell of sulfur fills the yard as he stumbles away,
each memory filling footprints he leaves:
boat holding water   tobacco juice   floating on the surface
minnows in the dark   dented tacklebox   rusting in the water

                        His crooked gait
takes him closer to the root of storm.
Night refuses to give way. He cannot blink
for each glinting flash reminds him of the line's strict tug

from the black water: the fish his father
made him take from the hook, cut open, and throw back.

BAD LUCK CRADLESONG

Do what you will with those pictures of your first lover:
the wind still bangs a screen door off its hinges
and simple myths, like mirrors, will continue to bootlick
the back of your mind. It seems natural to fall in love
at a funeral, a body shivering under weight,
those drinks staining the collars of your shirts.
Look all you want, you can laugh into the face of oblivion,
you can turn it on, turn it off again. Staring at the sun
will take your vision, and the light will be infinitely
repeating. When your sight seems to go, stare hard at nothing,
think of the dirt in your body. It will be light again.

Bad Luck Cradlesong (2)

Wonder, you think, ripped the heart from the rooster,
taught the fish to take the hook. Recall the blunder
of birth? The storm of urine in a bucket? Patience
requires a pause, tosses itself from the table
your lip makes, and loses itself in the woods,
the smoldering ash of memory. You place a rock
in place of the missing. The missing make room for you.

Bad Luck Cradlesong (3)

Can't see the field for the easel. Sometimes the easel
is a mirror and you're fixing your hair. Sometimes this eddy
of air carries the canvas into the woods, the tongue of a bear
in your pocket. Chasing it, you stop and think:
those trees contain a form I might someday admire
or *this bathtub has been the place of many a good weep*
and all apply as grasshoppers swarm around your face
until the sound of a yodel streams from inside a tree. Yes,
that is the curve of a lover you see in the shadow
of that tree, mossy blonde hair on the small
of her back. Her thighs and youth have turned to bark.

ROCKY SPRINGS

A longing inside the mind: to live in the past
as the person you are now. The moon is a paint bucket
on its side. You've spent all night erasing names
and details from letters, filling the gaps with origami birds.
The radio reminds you of falling in the woods on your back
and the way the sky looked through those loblolly pines,
the night so bird-less that worms could be heard digging,
the dance that felt new and routine and in disarray:
these are things no one else can know.

DOMINION

Things in miniature form seem oddly obtainable. When I held her tiny porcelain hand in mine, I thought she was an eternal object meant for greatness in the coastal cities of the world. Pessoa, with his path of feathers, understood this idea of objectification—love for one's self eases with the creation of many selves. Frenzied daydreams and a lack of grief pervades the element of innovation. Innovation is simply the act of placing something on your head that was never meant to be a hat.

SONG MADE OF ROPE

Laughing like a paper airplane or a soapbox derby when a wheel rolls off and the road turns to gravel, laughs change and rewind into clearing throats. Borges' blind eyes once imagined a bird eating another bird. His laugh, a skull bleaching in the sun, a painter inside-out, color caving in on itself, music in columns on eyelids, sip of water in a bored mouth, holding the banjo strings in place.

APOLOGY IN THE
SHADOW OF A SAIL

Often considered the caution of whales,
the sad stretch of water   —

where a metaphor dances on a grain of sand
and dies. A stand-still caution? A lighthouse?

I cannot stare into a tower of Babel with one idea
sleeping in the saddle of many tongues.

　　　My right hand will not hold a fork or tie any knots.

By saying a male bird cannot help but sing, you followed

each of my words to their beginning, even
now during the mourning period
when we ought to let silence strum its song.

　　　If you are sick at sea, remember the horizon, a hand-rail,
an arrow into the face of God.

　　　　　A male bird cannot help but sing

A male bird cannot help but sing

　　　A male bird cannot help but sing

and softly add to the confusion.

REASON

Watching the bones of heaven flash in the sky,
I remember the hotel in Kansas City,
the one that opened up to the train station
across the street and downtown blurred
by fog. I couldn't see the buildings,
only the lights, and the shadows of my mind
moved to make room for what I saw: all things
vilified when replaced with something else,
beautiful or not. Of the few things I've done,
I haven't done right, but when I looked out
from that hotel at the fog and tried to open the window,
it would not open for a reason—not for the padlock,
but for the sheer joy of memory: that vision
of heaven, blinking, at the top of a building.

Heard

I wish to applaud.

I wish to applaud so the sound
my palms make will rise to a place
more persistent than this one.

Aside from the urge
to disrupt else-
where, my resolve
for silence creates a silo
for any who would enter.

Instead, this new
stillness sighs itself
to eternal sleep. The dead
do not know who I am.

Prayer for Winter Solstice

The dark hand is a hand I love when the horizon of trusses
spreads out from the city, streams into the sky.

Even the fog cannot stop the flight of planes to the North,
even elegies spoken years ago blend into this pre-dawn black
and I am sure that, alone, Christ once looked into a well
and saw nothing.

        That same oblivion now stares down on the city
and through the boards on this pier. This reminds me
to give breath its rhythm.

        This reminds me of walking the tracks
over a river bed and thinking the past is cursed to bury
what it will. Tonight, let the dead bury the dead
with what hours are left and let the spoken word,
the voice of this season, replace the hum of this machine called flight.

FROM ESSEX

Now is the time to take the song from your throat
and unbury the bone you've tasted for years. The flesh
of bones is that which burdens the voice, the flesh
that feeds from the unspoken words in your throat
urging you not to pocket the flowers. Plunder
the scream of shades. Take the swarm of color
from the fields until the lack of color
forms a rupture in the sky and plunder
all unheard sounds in the night. These sounds
are yours. Your mind holds the morning back.
This voice whispers each word back
to you and each stone you gather slows sound
and light. The bleached day urges you on and the throat
of the lapwing burns black with still no sound.

III.

A Tiny Archway of Countless Songs

An Interjection

Barbershop chairs revolving in a junkyard. World's strongest
bed-frame, broken. O how I

loved you. The skeleton of clouds dripped its worst on us
as you said it would

with me dressed in my doubt.

       With winter so soon I have compiled notes on freezing

                   and think the geography
of weather to be everywhere and nowhere,
floating over a gray landscape with no cows, no
fucking. Your floral arrangements were beautiful.

Apology

Rivers are a savior   of sorts
My luck rests   in a river bed wrecked by coal

ON WATER

The clothes tossing for two hours. Your face
against the glass.

Crossing the water twice
toward home, the wash still turning:

a reminder that what occurs
on both sides of a river is inseparable.

Eternal apostrophes sailing eastward
on the ocean. And no one knows.

Everything done
already.

So fury burns on,
even in water,
but fury has two sides.

With my glass emptied and turned over,
I kiss the bottom

and lift my face to find you,
still and framed in its clouded circle.

NOCTURNE

O the banjo strings in me buzz
for you, Biblical one. Nest of nightmares. Nay-
sayers. Nothing, they are. All gone. Your tightrope
is wide and tickles me deep. The earthenworn
disasters are left to shards of ice
in the glassy flesh of our drinks.
O kiss of liquor, O swarm of skin,
tumble into one certain swing of revival.
If one of us is to stand on the appaloosa
shore among the rocks to guide
the dark ships to this river,
let the polish of your touch strip the color
from my skin. Swaddle your face
in a sleepy vision of shade and light.

ELEGY FOR THE SELF-PORTRAIT

Can there be more than one voice? I say these
words and hear you speak them. You hypothesize
that when tracing the path of our words
to sentences, we will find the thoughts
arrive from the same grassed-over cave

(I am platonically in love with my new best friend).

The piano we moved upstairs still sounds tuneless
and worn. *History hums one song*, I offer as
consolation for our bad backs. History assumes
a present and future—an urge to look
at the past and reason it good.

But the past
gains weight

and a burden
is born

in the waste
of its birth,

a burden
is born

in the depths
of its worth.

Destiny is a funny cap. In their consistency,
the seasons teach us that

all tired eyes are eventually
tossed into the yoke of Winter,
that blind canvas,
a tiny archway of countless songs.

In our home, hidden from the sky,
the light exceeds itself
because it will not be let in.

A home is shriveled, not scorned.

In the home movie of you during the holidays,
your eyes look as if they're hiding something.

It doesn't matter. It never mattered.

Ask and I will be your cuckoo for two hundred years.

One winter I saw a snowman
dressed like me,

a certain swell of light where his figure dwelt.

It confused me until I realized
you made the snowman for me.

I apologize for failing to see the humor of your action.

Ten laughs in the space where one should be.

The trees still bent from this winter's ice.
The joke of ten thousand years retreats
to the debris of its own punchline.
Tomorrow figures to be the passion of dirt.
Today is a bucket around which this house is built.

From humor comes history:

scrapes turned to bruises, fruit
rotting in the trash, the stutter
of firecrackers and words, dry
coffee in a cup, the Middle Fork
swollen to obscurity with mud,
threatened roads,

the sky so blue it crowds us near the ground.

Why do you still stand over the wash
watching the clothes
toss in the wake of soap and water?

Your mother is not there.
Your mother is in Nebraska,
a land of antique weather and resolute pianos.

Light ties all action to thought and builds a world
where music grows infinitely quiet in its eaves.

Yes, the pianos are quiet, yet they remain
consistent even in their silence.

(I know I am repeating myself)

Your floral arrangements were beautiful.

The children were, too. The window was so clean
I walked into it, hoping for a headfull of sky.

Today I crawled under our house.
Today I shined my flashlight
through a tiny hole in the floor

and saw your face staring back.

The creaking of the world
creaked on in the light
and I was a spider in the dark,
not yet light,
but bread becoming light.

Lost among those shards of ice
in our drinks on the dash.

Once this faucet was the shadow
of our collective, lyrical memory.

The night is a group of gathered vanishing points.

The narrative of sparrows will harden
                              to dawn.

BENEATH THE BRIDGE

The dead shepherd. The little river. The fields.
The cities. The hills of the world. Those that sleep
on the hills. Those that drink from the river.

Nightly I kneeled by that river when I lived in the city,
thought *some ballad singer had sung it all*
and each nocturnal note rhymed into the ground,
rhymed into the dark sarcophagus of sound.

It's only now that I realize I was wrong.
How often I was when I lived in the city.

Once in the shadow of an old bridge,
I met a gravedigger who had not heard this river.

He did not know where his family had gone.

He said: the radio of eternity begins anew
when each of us are born and ends each time
we look to the sky and think to sing along.

ABOUT THE AUTHOR

Adam Clay's poems have appeared in *Denver Quarterly*, *The Iowa Review*, *Barrow Street*, *Black Warrior Review*, *Fascicle*, *CutBank*, *The New Orleans Review*, *Conduit*, *Octopus Magazine*, *Free Verse*, and elsewhere. A chapbook, *Canoe*, is available from Horse Less Press. Born and raised in Mississippi, he earned an MFA from the University of Arkansas and an MA from The Center for Writers at The University of Southern Mississippi.

Photograph of Adam Clay. © 2006 by Kimberley Clay. Used by permission

FREE VERSE EDITIONS

Edited by Jon Thompson

2006

Physis by Nicolas Pesque, translated by Cole Swensen
Puppet Wardrobe by Daniel Tiffany
These Beautiful Limits by Thomas Lisk
The Wash by Adam Clay

2005

A Map of Faring by Peter Riley
Signs Following by Ger Killeen
Winter Journey [*Viaggio d'inverno*] by Attilio Bertolucci, translated by Nicholas Benson

Printed in the United States
60379LVS00004B/118-171